OUR HOLY YEARNINGS

JOAN CHITTISTER

OUR HOLY YEARNINGS

Life Lessons for Becoming Our Truest Selves

For more information
about Joan Chittister, OSB,
please visit her website:
www.joanchittister.org

TWENTY-THIRD PUBLICATIONS
A Division of Bayard
One Montauk Avenue, Suite 200
New London, CT 06320
(860) 437-3012 or (800) 321-0411
www.23rdpublications.com

ISBN 978-1-62785-046-9
Library of Congress Control Number: 2014947510

Printed in the U.S.A.

·⇒ CONTENTS ⇐·

I looked for that which is not, nor can be,
And hope deferred made my heart sick in truth;
But years must pass before a hope of youth
Is resigned utterly.
CHRISTINA ROSSETTI

The poet Christina Rossetti points to the truth it can take a lifetime to learn: that what we get in life is far too often not what we're looking for at all. But we can and often do go on looking, regardless. Then, years later, having looked in all the wrong places, we at last discover that it is letting go of all those things that finally frees us. Then we come to understand that it is the looking itself that is of the essence of the spiritual life.

The pursuit of human fulfillment drives us from one thing to another, yearning, relinquishing, and searching again. It nips at our heels, prompting us down the twists and turns of life, inexorably, indomitably, until, exhausted, we finally learn to settle for what is, rather than go on seeking what we think we must have but never find.

In the meantime, between those two points in life, between the looking and end of looking, we stretch ourselves to the ultimate lengths of the self. We go through fatigue and confusion to the very edges of despair in our unquenchable thirst for more. The soul simply refuses to cease the fruitless search for what is not in the land of What Is.

And the world around us is only too happy to feed our needs.

We want to be beautiful, so the ads promise us beauty. But under everything they sell us, we remain forever the same. We want to be wealthy, so the stock market and the lottery and the bank offer us money. But when the numbers come in and the costs go out, we are no richer now than we were before. We want to be successful, but when we achieve success, we either fail to recognize it or refuse to consider it enough. There is, we are sure, more and more and more.

So perfection doesn't work, because it can't be achieved. Failure we take as total loss and lose heart for the rest of life. Humility we confuse with humiliation and avoid it like the plague. Entertainment we mistake for joy and wonder why it doesn't last.

But then, if we're lucky, the confusion dissolves in us. We begin to understand. And all the disappointments in life become more bearable as we go. They come to hurt less, to trouble us less and less. We begin to realize that there is more to yearning than simply wanting what doesn't exist. Yearning, in fact, is the holy sign that we are made for more than the apparent, the tenuous, the temporary. We begin to know now that nothing in life can ever satisfy the human need for the eternally incomplete, the tinker toys of life.

Yearning is what tells us that we are made for holiness. Yearning is holiness itself in disguise. It keeps us looking for the God who is Complete Satisfaction. For the God who is Everything. For the God in whom we lack nothing and because of whom everything else pales into the nothingness it is.

And when we finally discover that God is all that really is, that nothing else can ever satisfy, that everything else is empty however full we want it to be, we are finally home.

Then, life sinks into Mindfulness. Darkness, we find, is only the invitation to Light. Enlightenment comes: everything we wanted and did not get was only prelude to what it means to want nothing but the Good. And when that happens, behold—we suddenly recognize that we have had everything all the while.

Indeed, as Rossetti writes, "Years must pass before a hope of youth / Is resigned utterly." Indeed, the yearning is unending and the search is eternal. But in the end, as the soul matures, it is the yearning itself for Everything, for the Fullness of Life, that saves us.

I wanted a perfect ending...Now I've learned,
the hard way, that some poems don't rhyme, and some
stories don't have a clear beginning, middle,
and end....Delicious ambiguity.

GILDA RADNER

Perfection

In those days, absolutely everything about the marriage was wrong: She was Catholic; he was Protestant. She was a young widow; he had never been married. She had a child whom he adopted, but he loved children and wanted his own. That never happened. Both of their families lived in the north of the state. Because of his work, they moved to its very southern edge where there were no cousins, no aunts, no family. She sent the child to a Catholic school; his Protestant mother did not approve. She wanted the husband to become Catholic; he didn't. The tensions were everywhere.

So, one day I said, "Mother, tell me about my real father." She looked at me long and hard. "You have a father," she said to me. "I know," I said. "But I want to know what my own father was like." She thought a moment. "Joan, your father was very young when he died. I have no idea what he would have been like had he lived, and I don't want you idolizing a myth." I was ten years old. "But, Momma," I argued, "we would all have been Catholic and that would have been better." I was the only child in my class with a Protestant father, and I was clearly tired of explaining to people how such a strange thing could ever have happened. "Joan," she said firmly, "life goes on. We don't know why your father died. That is for a reason that we can't understand yet. But we do know that God is in it with us. That's all we need to know. There is nothing else to say." And she didn't.

But if it had not been for that strangely skewed beginning, I know when I look back, my own life would never have developed the way it has. The insight that life is about "now" could never have come so young. The awareness of otherness would not have come for years—maybe never. The understanding of what it means to be different and marginal—light years ahead on some things, completely out of it on others—might never have seared and stretched my soul. I might have grown up thinking that I was normative, that everybody was supposed to look like us, that anybody who didn't was inferior or bad or out of step. I might have grown up thinking that only Catholics went to heaven. But with a laughing Protestant grandfather and a loving Protestant stepfather, I learned young that that couldn't be true, wasn't true, would never be true.

As Gilda Radner says, my life wasn't neat; it didn't evolve the way the social scripts said it should. There was no clear beginning, middle, or end. It was not "The-Catholic-Family-of-the-Year" story. But it was just what I needed. Both then and now. And so, in the end, is everybody's life, I think.

The sad thing is thinking that there's something perfect against which we must model ourselves—and then fail to meet it.

"Perfection" is the neurosis of those who believe that life was made for us to control rather than to grow into. No, life is not about becoming perfect. It is about becoming whole, becoming complete, becoming fully alive human beings. And that is never "perfect." That is messy to the max.

·⇾⇾⇾⇽⇽⇽·

Perfect is a warped shadow of what really is. Life consists of twists and turns, a maze of possibilities through which we wind our way to becoming everything we are.

There is a difference between the perfect and the desirable. Perfect is a plastic imitation of the real, a counterfeit attempt to reproduce someone else's definition of life or standards. The desirable, on the other hand, is an attempt to make the imperfect just a little better. "It is reasonable," Samuel Johnson wrote, "to have perfection in our eye that we may always advance toward it, though we know it can never be reached."

P erfect imitations of past pieces of new awareness are not art. "The artist who aims at perfection in everything," Delacroix wrote, "achieves it in nothing."

Perfection, whatever there is of it in life, is not always as holy as it seems. Too often perfection comes more out of ego than it does out of commitment.

Perfection is the end of a process, not its beginning. That's why they call it experience.

In our compulsion to be perfect, we have driven ourselves to the point where silver medals, the thousandths of a second between athletes on an Olympic podium, have become more a sign of failure than they are of success. How warped can we get? "No good work whatever can be perfect," John Ruskin wrote, "and the demand for perfection is always a sign of a misunderstanding of the ends of art."

When we realize what we lack, we are ready to join the rest of the human race. "This is the very perfection of a person," Augustine wrote, "to find out our own imperfections."

Beware the temptation to find yourself perfect. That is the day you will find yourself dead—either of body or of soul.

Perfection is not possible on earth, so why do we insist on measuring ourselves by its standards? We set ourselves up only to be disappointed in ourselves or jealous of others.

When I am intent only on being perfect in life, I lose the joy that comes from learning to fail freely. Then, as Tennyson says, I run the risk of becoming "faultily faultless, icily regular, splendidly null, dead perfection; no more."

If God expected perfection, would we have been created in the first place? Learning to accept the theology of failure is a far safer road to heaven than the theology of perfection will ever be.

The purpose of my imperfections is to enable me to live well, to act kindly, to be loving with others.

When we drive ourselves to be perfect, we drive ourselves to exhaustion, to temper, to disappointment and a sense of failure. We forget the simple joy of being alive. "Perfectionism," said Hugh Prather, "is slow death." Relax. Just give yourself a break.

Having a goal to aim at is a good thing; requiring of ourselves that we make it, on the other hand, is deadly. "Ideals are like the stars," Carl Schurz said. "We never reach them, but like the mariners of the sea, we chart our course by them."

If we insist on everything in life being perfect, we doom ourselves to unhappiness. Better to find the joy of the nearly good enough than exhaust ourselves on the impossible. "I dance to the tune that is played," the Spanish say. It's the grace to go on dancing, whatever the tune, that counts.

To say that a thing is perfect is to say that it cannot be improved upon. How boring. "Growth," John Henry Newman wrote, "is the only evidence of life we have."

2

What God gave Adam was not forgiveness from sin.
What God gave Adam was the right to begin again.
ELIE WIESEL

We Fall and We Get Up

We live at a very strange moment in history. A confluence of peoples, cultures, customs, and moral standards makes us all more aware than ever of our own mores and precepts. But few groups of people anywhere, anymore, can assume that the standards of their group will be the sole standard of the nation in which they live.

Nor have they ever been, incidentally. In this country, for instance, we have always had a Protestant/Catholic dichotomy. We have honored and respected the multiple traditions of Judaism, Islam, Buddhism, and Hinduism that have sprung up among us. The Amish and Mennonites have for centuries lived in our midst, a highly moral people who express their morality differently from most of the rest of the United States. We have watched group after group of immigrants adjust to being "American" and yet remain true to their own religious rituals and rules at the same time.

Obviously, it is possible for a diverse population to agree on common standards of the public good and civic standards while they themselves continue to operate out of their own particular ethical and religious frameworks.

So, what does it really mean now, as the ancient spiritual "Work of Mercy" counsels us, to "admonish the sinner"? Surely it does not mean that we must see that everybody else be like us. And yet, unless we do, how can we possibly correct ethical abuse in a pluralistic society?

There was a time when prisons set out to be rehabilitative institutions. They provided the job training, spiritual counsel, and educational background prisoners lacked in order to be better human beings as well as citizens in the future. Now we warehouse prisoners without the personal or spiritual resources human development demands till their terms expire or DNA tests prove their innocence. Then we release them no more prepared to live the life ahead of them now than they were in the past.

Point: To admonish the sinner requires that, as a society, we do more than punish people who violate our common civic standards. We need to do more than criticize the sin or condemn the sinner to one kind of social exclusion or the other. We must provide the educational systems, the social support structures, and the criminal justice system it will take to define what is socially desirable for the entire society and make it personally attainable.

Before we "admonish the sinner," in other words, we need to admonish ourselves a bit for what we are failing to provide for those we are admonishing.

Human failure is a very human thing. It is common to us all. What is not common is that we allow it to rule us. "What do you do in a monastery?" a disciple asked the old monastic. And the monastic answered simply, "We fall and we get up and we fall and we get up and we fall and we get up again." It is the "getting up" that requires help.

We are all capable of being better than we are. But for most of us that requires good formation, kind attention, loving correction, and the desire to succeed.

Conscience is the voice that reminds us that we have not lived up to our own best ideals. The psychologist Carl Jung wrote: "Deep down below the surface of the average conscience a still, small voice says to us, 'Something is out of tune.'"

Good development requires that we have good friends, friends who themselves listen for the voice of God in life. Or, as Abraham Lincoln put it, "Stand with anybody that stands right. Stand with them while they are right and part with them when they go wrong."

Learning to choose good from good and best from better is the highest achievement of the human spirit.

Failure is not fatal. In fact, it is failure that enables us to grow. It gives a reason to begin again.

When we begin to own our errors, when we begin to take responsibility for our mistakes, we will have become adults. Then, we become spiritually mature.

Sin is the sign that something is missing in our lives. "All sins are attempts to fill voids," Simone Weil wrote. Admonishment will only work, then, when we know what we're really looking for—and pursue it instead.

To make a sin undesirable is far more important than simply punishing people for doing it. The United States has five percent of the population of the world and twenty-five percent of its prisoners. Clearly our prison systems don't work. Isn't it time to ask ourselves why?

When "accuse" and "admonish," "punish" and "rehabilitate" become synonyms, it is clear that a society is failing in its responsibility—both to the victim and to the victimizer.

Sin is a function of being human. We are not perfect, and we fail. But sin is a teacher. We learn when we sin that the purpose of time is to repent, to do better, to trust in God's mercy. "Sin, in a way," Charles Handy wrote, "is God's gift to humanity."

Only when we lose hope in the mercy of God and in our own genuine determination to do better have we really abandoned ourselves to living a life beneath God's will for us. "It is more serious," John of Carpathos wrote, "to lose hope than to sin."

There is one holy goal in life: to refuse to make life more difficult for others than it already is. Then, if I can truly do that, the difficulties of my own life can only disappear.

When we say "that's just the way I am," we abandon fullness of life for fullness of the present moment. In the light of eternity, that is, at best, a very bad bargain.

However animalistic a human being acts, treating them like animals will never make full human beings out of them, no matter how many years we try.

It can take a long time to become the person we really want to be. As Mary Pickford writes, "You may have a fresh start any moment you choose, for this thing we call 'failure' is not the falling down, it is the staying down."

·⊸ 3 ⊷·

If upon awakening your first thought
is of God, you are a monk.
WAYNE TEASDALE

The Sacred Quest

Every one of us is hardwired for God. The
data are clear: We know our incompleteness.
We recognize our emptiness. We live with a
sense of continual desire and unending dis-
satisfaction. And so we walk the paths of life
like a Geiger counter waiting for the signal
that tells us we have finally grasped the invis-
ible, the ungraspable, the Whole.

We search ceaselessly for the more of life, contented but not fulfilled. We live with expectations of tomorrow, and then find tomorrow not enough as well. We struggle with our restlessness today. We go through life with the magnet in our souls that is meant to bring us home, wherever, in the end, home really is.

It is that reaching out into the nowhere looking for the everything that makes every one of us, as Wayne Teasdale says, "a monk."

There is, for each of us, an unseeable star in life that we follow, often to false ends. We follow the star to money, but when we get the money, what we buy with it fails to fill the breach between having and wanting. We follow the star to success, but today's pinnacle is only tomorrow's memory. We follow the star to one person and then another, but, good, captivating, inspiring as they may be, none of them really fills the great gullet of the soul for long.

Then, if we live long enough, think about it deeply enough, face the problem honestly enough, we finally understand: we are born to be discontented.

Oh, life makes us happy, yes, but satisfied, no. We have here a taste of what fullness of life is meant to be, but, at the same time, there is nothing here that quenches the thirsts or fills all the cravings. What we have here is only the hint of what we are meant to become.

At that point, we must begin to listen to the call within. We must begin to ask ourselves what it is that undergirds everything we do, every thought we think, every step we take.

The monastic life builds the idea of the whole of life into daily life. There are regular moments of daily prayer, regularly scheduled times of sacred readings, regular periods of annual retreat, meant to bind both parts of life—spiritual and professional—together, regular interruptions in the day designed to keep fresh the idea that, whatever we do, every step we take in life is simply another step on the way to God.

Everything, the monastic knows, begins and ends with God: thought, work, relationships, goals, and purpose. God becomes the rhythm of the day, the first thought on waking, the last thought at night, the reason for everything we do in life. The monastic lives in a weather vane world that points always and only toward God.

The monastic heart is the heart that concentrates solely, consciously, completely on living this life in the womb of God, in the essence of the eternal one. When God is the "monos," the only goal of our lives, then we are living a "monastic" life, whatever the shape—married, single, or religious—the monastery of my own particular soul-life may be.

When God becomes conscious to each of us, when we direct our lives to that consciousness, when that consciousness is the undercurrent of every thought and word and action of our lives, then we know that Brother Wayne is startlingly correct: then "you are a monk."

·᠔᠔᠔᠆᠐᠐᠐᠆

Americans are very pragmatic people. If we want something, we never doubt that we can figure out how to go about getting it. It never occurs to us, however, that there are some things that are not meant to be achieved. God, in fact, is one of those things. If God can be gotten, then God is not God. In this case, it is the search itself that is the finding.

The God-search is the pulse that drives us from one thing to another in life and gives us the wisdom to choose between them.

An awareness of God comes from the ever-ungratified outreach of the soul. We are not meant to be satisfied in this life, only to be aware that not everything is to be found here.

"All I ever wanted was to sing to God," Peter Shaffer wrote. "God gave me that longing and then made me mute." It is the discovery that nothing here ever really squelches the thirst of the soul that, in the end, finally leads us, exhausted and grateful, to God.

Just when we think we have no spiritual life at all may be exactly the moment when the seed for one has begun to take root in us.

We are born with God pulsing through our veins. The rest of life is simply the process of coming to realize that nothing else we make God will ever be able to be God for us.

The search for God comes one day to the point where we know without doubt that we are immersed in God. Bringing ourselves to finally recognize that is the essential task of life.

There is no such thing as "getting" God. The fact is that we already have God. It is the awareness of that presence that life intends to teach us to cultivate. Samuel Beckett writes, "Given the existence of a personal God who loves us dearly, it is established beyond all doubt that humanity wastes and pines for reasons unknown."

The God of Light is also the God of Darkness. Why would we not expect God, then, to be in the dark spots of our lives as well as in its light?

Most of life is spent trying to make our own gods. Then, when they fail us, as all of them do, we discover underneath it all that God has been there all the time.

God is not dead. God is simply waiting for us in silence so that, in touch with God ourselves, we can be the voice of the love of God to others.

Prayer is much more than "prayers." It is awareness, attention, and presence. "Certain thoughts are prayers," Victor Hugo wrote. "There are moments when, whatever be the attitude of the body, the soul is on its knees."

God is not an occasional find in life—in church, maybe, or at sunset. God is a sense of life now and of life beyond life. God is what carries me through life. God is what calls me to live for more than the present, to live despite the past, to live into the heart of the universe.

God is not somewhere else. God is everywhere. God is here. With me. In me. Now. "We have what we seek," the monk Thomas Merton wrote. "We don't have to rush after it. It was there all the time, and if we give it time, it will make itself known to us."

Once we begin to recognize God at work in us, everything in life becomes holy, becomes life-giving.

The presence of God in our lives affects everything else about it; it focuses our values; it directs our desires; it shapes our relations to others; it simplifies our needs.

··❧ 4 ❧··

Do your work, then step back.
The only path to serenity.
Lao Tzu

The Power
of Humility

One of the most impacting spiritual posters of
the twentieth century was not published by a
church. It came out of the Special Olympics
and it was the air-pumping picture of a youth
with Down syndrome who had just finished a

race—dead last. His face was aglow. His eyes shone. His smile was full to bursting the confines of his face. He had done what he set out to do. He had become all he could in the doing of it. He had stretched himself to the limits of the self and, as a result, became an icon for the rest of the world to measure themselves by as well.

He had done his work and then stepped away from it. It was not the measure of his entire life. It was not his sign of triumph over others. It was the sign only of the fullness of himself.

As far as we know, he was never seen publicly again. No newspaper stories. No photographs. No scenes of celebration follow him now. He simply left the arena of public display—happy, satisfied, fulfilled, and measured only by his own goals. He did what he had come to do and then disappeared back into himself to go on becoming in hundreds of other ways. He did not make a business of the self.

In a society given to neon signs, football trophies, celebrity reality shows, and "top ten" lists for everything, there is little limelight left over for the likes of Chinese poets who preach the distance between what we are and what we do. Lao Tzu's type of person lives too quiet to be heard, too small to be seen, too gentle to be noticed. But too important to be overlooked. These people teach us our own importance. More than that, they teach us to make a distinction between what we do and what we are. They teach us to live rather than to do.

In our culture, on the other hand, importance is expressed in the singular: we lionize the one person to win six triathlons in a row, for instance. Or the only person to scale a given mountain. Or the first person to fly around the globe in a balloon. We make people what they do.

As a result of our concentration on the

achievement and competition that come from uniqueness, we are inclined to overlook the uniqueness of simplicity. We downplay the power of humility. We ignore the impact of the individual. We merge the person and the things they do to the point where we are in danger of losing a sense of the person at all.

Then we wonder why it is that loss destroys people and pride consumes them and humility puzzles us.

But at the end of the day, we discover that humility—the strength to separate our sense of the meaning of life from what we do—is the only real answer to lifelong happiness.

It's the incessant social demand for achievement and power, control and celebrity, that erodes the spirit. It creates generations of strivers without cause, of the ambitious who are unsatisfied with life. It is a social virus, a plague that infects the whole culture. And it begins young. Children of five are goaded and prodded by parents as well as coaches to win Little League games before they can barely hold a bat.

Competition infects every dimension of society: education, business, politics, play. Nothing is done for its own sake. Everything is done to win something, to get something, to best someone else, to prove the value of everyone in sight: young people, corporate leaders, political figures, athletes who would just as soon play the game for the sake of playing rather than consume their lives and sacrifice their bodies for the sake of winning. It's the comparative value of a person that counts in a society such as this, not the personality or the character or the morality or the simple deep-down goodness of people committed to, as St. Philippine Duchesne put it, "simple duty daily done."

Instead, the society breeds a pathological pride for its need to succeed. And, as a result, it nurtures a pride far beyond the healthy joy of those who have done their best; it leads to a pride that in its devotion to mastery, to recognition, to superiority, agitates the proud to the point of despair. It makes them fierce seekers of advantage in everything, and it infuriates them when they lack that advantage. It leaves them, ironically, losers on the levels that, in the end, are the only ones that really count.

·⚜⚜⚜·

Only the humble are truly happy. There is nothing they have that anyone can take from them, and all that they have, whatever it is, they enjoy for its own sake. "True humility," Henri Frederic Amiel wrote, "is contentment."

Humility, the ability to go through life with open hands and an accepting heart, is the gift that enables a person to survive anything and everything. "Humility," George Arliss wrote, "is the only true wisdom by which we prepare our minds for all the possible changes of life."

There is a good and healthy pride that takes more pleasure in the aspiration—in the desire to do good and do it well—than in the achievement itself.

The truly humble never really covet recognition. They simply accept it, if and when it comes, and wear it lightly.

Humility is the foundation of humanity. It is the glue that binds a group together, aware of their own gifts, grateful for the gifts of others.

National pride is a necessary dimension of national development. National arrogance is an unfortunate dimension that leads to national diminishment.

Humility frees us from the burden of perfection.

The humble person learns more than other people. "The greatest friend of Truth," Charles Caleb Colton wrote, "is Time, her greatest enemy is Prejudice, and her constant companion is Humility."

Humility is about bringing life to everything we do—and then letting it become its own thing. As Margaret Mead put it, "And when our baby stirs and struggles to be born it compels humility: What we began is now its own."

The beauty of education is that it teaches us how little we know. Education is the seedbed of humility.

Pride focuses on externals. Humility springs from an internal well. "We're so engaged in doing things to achieve purposes of outer value," Joseph Campbell writes, "that we forget the inner value; the rapture that is associated with being alive is what it is all about."

Humility is the height of inner freedom. It is in thrall to no one and nothing, not even its own self-image. "When we lose the right to be different," Charles Evans Hughes wrote, "we lose the privilege to be free."

The smug are the shallow. They have yet to learn what qualities they lack and so have little chance of supplying them for themselves.

Humility frees us to think again, to rethink old thoughts, to think new thoughts openly, to make the mistakes that grow us. "Freedom is not worth having," Gandhi wrote, "if it does not connote freedom to err."

When all we have to think about is ourselves and our own accomplishments, we have exhausted a very small library indeed. "Woe to those," Abba Silvanus taught, "whose reputation is greater than their work."

Natural gifts are made to be given, cannot be denied, and are the deepest kind of humility. "You can muffle the drum," Kahlil Gibran wrote, "and you can loosen the strings of the lyre, but who shall command the skylark not to sing?"

·◦→ 5 ←◦·

For everything that lives is holy, life delights in life.
WILLIAM BLAKE

Pure Reverence

In Tokyo, the side streets are barely more than cemented single-lane footpaths. They wind aimlessly back into the bowels of the city. Not a slice of sky separates one building from another down these narrow, sinuous ways. Back there, the density of population, the smothering admixture of architecture from totally distinct historical periods, and the very concentration of people and buildings crowd the spirit.

But inside the new and towering skyscrapers, it is different. Tiny Japanese gardens, fountains flowing, draw visitors into intricate patterns of rock gardens and fish-filled canals that wind their way past miniature temples, around mounds of manicured grasses, and through bantam copses of toy trees. The gardens touch up against the sterile offices that surround them, stilling all the noise, giving soul to the crush of humanity that pours through the commercial center of the city.

Unlike their Japanese counterparts, the lobby and core of a skyscraper in the United States is commonly spacious, filled with furniture and displays, service centers, and a confluence of coffee shops and lunch counters, gift stores, and banquet rooms. What they do not have that the Japanese provide for assiduously is emptiness.

The meeting place for our session in Tokyo, they told me, was through the double doors to the left of the elevator. I was not surprised to find the elevator padded with brass-studded leather. The fact that the carpet in the corridor was thick and soft seemed usual enough. The real surprise, however, was that beyond the heavy oak doors, the meeting room was not the average conference room of large round tables and fold-up metal chairs flung from one end of the room to the other. Instead, there was nothing in this maroon and gold draped room but one needle-nosed red celadon vase that held one fresh yellow rose. One rose in one vase on a glass table in the middle of a room draped in red and gold velvet. Nothing but pure mindfulness, pure reverence, pure life. This room, you had to think, had been built for this one vase and this single rose. The stark attention, the sentinel awareness, the utterly concentrated focus on one rose steeped the room in the consciousness of beauty.

·⤞⤞⤞⤝⤝⤝··

Mindfulness, the awareness of the sacredness of the details of life, makes haste and trumpery impossible. It makes every act a sacred act.

Details are the small things that make the important things important: the extra cherry on the birthday cake, the twist of the wrist in ballet, the deep blue in the painting, the cocked head on the dog. "Love's first step," the philosopher Simone Weil wrote, "is attention."

Learning to be outside in a world of inside activities is the ultimate spiritual freedom. The monastics of the desert tell a story about St. Antony.

"Abba," someone asked Antony, "how can you be enthusiastic when the comfort of books has been taken away from you?" And Antony replied, "My book, O Philosopher, is the nature of created things. Whenever I want to read the word of God, it is usually right in front of me."

Raised to think about the next world for the sake of religion, we far too often forget about this one for the sake of deepening our spirituality. But the writer Pearl Buck was not fooled. "I am so absorbed in the wonder of the earth and life upon it," she said, "that I cannot think of heaven and the angels. I have enough for this life."

The Creator is in the creation. Nikos Kazantzakis puts it this way: "God changes appearances every second. Blessed is the one who can recognize God in all God's disguises. One moment God is a glass of fresh water; the next, your son bouncing on your knees, or an enchanting woman, or perhaps merely a morning walk." Enjoy them all.

We know that we have lost touch with creation because we have come to the point where we can demolish it with cavalier abandon. "The more clearly we can focus our attention on the wonders and realities of the universe around us," Rachel Carson wrote, "the less taste we have for destruction."

How could it be that we
have come to spend
more time concentrating
on the life we left behind than on
the future we are creating for others?
"We do not inherit the earth from
our ancestors," a Native American
proverb reminds us, "we borrow it
from our children."

There is something lacking in the
soul of a people whose only time
frame is Now. There is an entire
dimension of life to be developed
in me if I have no care for what
has come to me from the past, no
concern for passing it on to the
future even better than I received it.

To recognize the beauty of the
natural saves us from swamping our

lives in the detritus of falsehood and pretense. One homely houseplant is worth all the plastic flowers in the world.

To turn a river into a cesspool, to use up the land by force-feeding it with chemicals that ironically leave it sterile in the end—this is to make ourselves God, a false one. "What good is a house," Henry David Thoreau wrote, "if you haven't got a tolerable planet to put it on?"

Nothing is more difficult than to appreciate the obvious—and nothing is more necessary on any level. "When the well's dry," Benjamin Franklin wrote, "we know the worth of water."

The wars of the next century, it is said, will not be fought over oil. They will be fought over water. But whether oil or water, both wars begin in us seeking more than we need. How can we possibly say that these issues have nothing to do with us? As Shakespeare says, "One touch of nature makes the whole world kin."

To be whole ourselves, we must make the effort it requires to understand what is happening to the world. Then, we must make the effort to change our own lives in ways that begin to reverse the damage.

Though we stand at the top of the food chain, the irony is that if the inability of nature to sustain life continues at its present rate, we will be the first to go. René J. Dubos warns us: "The belief that we can manage the Earth and improve on Nature is probably the ultimate expression of human conceit, but it has deep roots in the past and is almost universal."

Once people lived on the land. Now most people live in the cities. We have not only forgotten who we are but what we are. We are not only the part of nature that depends on the land, we are also the people on whom the land depends as well. It is the covenant of life—and we are breaking it.

We are all miracles living on a miracle called the Earth. It is only a matter of coming to recognize what that means, both to us and to the rest of the people of the world. Thich Nhat Hanh says of it, "The miracle is not to walk on water. The miracle is to walk on the green earth in the present moment, to appreciate the peace and beauty that are available now."

6

One joy dispels a hundred cares.

CONFUCIUS

Make Room for Joy

I can still see me standing there. Alone. Wary. Exhausted. Confused. And totally at the mercy of the universe. Oh, I know what Confucius is talking about all right.

It was my first international trip. I was on my way to Europe for a month, and it had already been grueling enough for all the regular reasons: While everyone else on the plane lay curled up in soft blankets for a bit of sleep before arrival, I never closed my eyes the entire night. Which meant that the time in Switzerland—going up and down mountain sides, getting on and off increasingly smaller trains with increasingly heavier luggage—got more and more difficult. The last thread snapped when the luggage cart, on which I'd hung my brand new camera while I jerked suitcases from it to the taxicab, turned up empty when I turned around to retrieve it.

Days later, when I got on the night train for Rome—where I would meet the travel companion who had all the information for the rest of the trip—the adventure had turned more than a little sour, and I had turned more than a little exhausted. Buy the ticket, watch the luggage; get to the train, drag the luggage; struggle up the railroad car steps; lift the luggage. It was all getting to be a bit too much.

This time I would surely sleep. I stacked the large bag in the little compartment, put my legs over it—just to be safe—snuggled up against the window, and went sound asleep. The next thing I heard was the conductor tapping me awake to punch my ticket. "No, no, no," the conductor was saying, his head shaking, a frown on his face. "What is no, no, no?" I said. He shook my ticket in my face. "No," he said again. This time more emphatically.

It took a while, but he got through to me when he began to push my luggage down the aisle toward the door. This train was going to Rome, all right, but my ticket was for another train. I was to get out of this one and wait for that one. The engine ground to a stop and I found myself, a foreign woman alone, at a small rural station in the dark of an Italian countryside at two in the morning. Two loud drunks ambled up and down the tracks shouting imprecations at no one in particular. Other than that, the little station was dark and empty. Completely, totally empty.

I went to the far end of the small platform,

dragging my heavy luggage beside me, tired, lost and—if truth were known—scared. I had no idea where I was or what to do next. I had no way to contact anyone for help, including the sister who was waiting for me to join her for the rest of the trip on another train. Somewhere. Sometime.

Thirty minutes, forty-five minutes, passed. Nothing. Except the drunks, of course, still stabbing at windmills in the air.

Then, out of the dark, an old woman, her husband, and a young teenage girl ambled on to the platform. They checked what I learned later was the travel board—but which I could not read—opened a brown paper bag, and took out their breakfast panini and cheese. The old man shooed the young drunks away with a shout and a sign.

Suddenly, spying me staring at them from the end of the overhang on the dark walkway, the old woman came down the platform, reached out her hand, hooked her arm through mine, and making the cooing sounds and little patter of mothers and sisters and girlfriends and aunts and grandmothers everywhere, simply walked me up the platform to be with the family for their little makeshift breakfast.

The joy, the relief, the gratitude of a lifetime washed over me in waves. It dissipated the terror I had been fighting down inside of me for hours.

How were Rome and Switzerland, the meetings and the audience with the pope, you ask? I don't have a clue. I don't remember another thing about it. The only sliver of memory left of that trip is that tight, caring grip on my arm, that still warm moment of pure unadulterated joy.

·-3-3-4-4-4-·

Joy is not a loud laugh. Joy is the quiet bubbling up, the overflow of the heart that knows it is at home in the universe.

Without joy, there is something wrong with everything we do. With joy, everything is possible.

We get back exactly the amount of joy we give in life. It all starts with me.

Fun is commonplace. Joy, like diamonds, is a rarer thing, indeed. It is the point at which all we know of security, peace, and contentment comes together in one significant wave. "I have diligently numbered the days of pure and genuine happiness which have fallen to my lot," Abd El Raham wrote. "They amount to fourteen."

In the midst of pain, do something good and joyful for yourself. It is important that we not let sorrow consume us. "I have an inward treasure born within me," Charlotte Brontë wrote, "which can keep me alive if all the extraneous delights should be withheld or offered only at a price I cannot afford."

Joy is the elixir of life. Joy is what enables us to remember all our dead loves with a smile for what they gave us rather than only the agony of losing them.

Those who do not cultivate joy in life never really know life. "People need joy," Margaret Collier Graham writes, "quite as much as clothing. Some of them need it far more."

Be certain to do something that gives you joy—reading, music, playing with the pet, holding the baby—at least once a day. It makes getting up the next day easier.

Two things most bind a group into a community: shared sorrow and shared joy. Never ignore either one of them. "The sharing of joy, whether physical, emotional, psychic, or intellectual," Audre Lorde teaches, "forms a bridge between the sharers which can be the basis for understanding much of what is not shared between them. It lessens the threat of their difference."

To live life on joys remembered rather than on joy in the here and now is to abandon the very meaning of "life."

Say to yourself a dozen times a day "I like this..."—whatever it is—and joy will begin to seep out of your very pores to everyone you meet. As Jean Webster writes, "It isn't the great big pleasures that count the most; it's making a great deal out of all the little ones."

Without pain we could never know the real meaning of joy. "A wounded deer," Emily Dickinson wrote, "leaps highest."

Beware the temptation to isolate yourself in order to avoid the kind of hurts that come from relationship, from risk. "The walls we build around us to keep sadness out," Jim Rohn writes, "also keep out the joy."

It is not the thing itself that brings us either joy or pain. It is the attitude we bring to it. The Buddhist monk Thich Nhat Hanh says of it, "Sometimes your joy is the source of your smile, but sometimes your smile can be the source of your joy."

Joy is not an exercise in perpetual giddiness. It is the practice of perpetual openness to life.

The person who is spiritually mature trusts in the presence of a loving God to bring this moment, whatever it is, to ripe in my soul. So as Pir Vilayet Khan says, "The only relevant spiritual question is: Why aren't you dancing with joy at this very moment?"

Joy is as much a responsibility—if not for the cultivation of my own joy, certainly for its presence in the life of those around me—as it is a gift. When we let go of getting or giving joy, we have abdicated our commitment to the goodness of life.

Remember the old saying, "Two men looked out through prison bars/ One saw mud, the other saw

71

stars"? Well, Abraham Lincoln put it this way: "Most folks are about as happy as they make up their minds to be."

7

When it is dark enough, you can see the stars.
RALPH WALDO EMERSON

Luminous Darkness

One of the interesting things about modern life is that almost nobody you talk to is where they started out thinking they would be at this point in their lives. And even then, almost nobody really sought to be where they now are. And yet, almost all of them are satisfied to be there.

And best of all, almost all of them are happy.

Correction: Almost all of them found happiness on the other side of unhappiness, the side of it they definitely would have avoided if only they could have.

Life is like that. It is the discovery of light in what seems to be the darkest of places, a coming to find the stars behind the clouds, the astonishing revelation of fullness where only emptiness seemed to be.

I met a woman recently, for instance, whose business failed. Went absolute bust. She was devastated and desperate. So she went back to school in slim hope of getting into some kind of skills training that would be recession-proof. Instead, she wound up as a corporate trainer. Her face glows when she tells the story of the failure that turned out to be her life's desire.

Then, I had supper with a woman who had been a successful teacher in a country in Central America. Her husband, a labor leader, found himself declared an enemy of the government, hunted down, in danger. If he wanted to save his life, he had to leave the country. At the same time, it was hard for her to even think of leaving—very hard. She had no desire whatsoever to come here, to lose her parents, her sisters, her professional position, her home, her friends, her country—her language even. But she was married. She had children. For her it was not a choice. Today she is a citizen with a stable job, her own home, new friends, a new future, a radiant smile, a strong character, and a look in her eye that tells not only of where she's been, but the joy of where she is.

Last week I was in a small group discussion on "Contemplation and the Modern World." The question was: "What is the place of contemplation, if any, in contemporary society?" Most of the answers were rooted in classic and traditional understandings of the contemplative approach to life. But one man took all the classic answers and made them real. "Two years ago," he said, "my wife and I lost everything:

our home, our investments, our property, our belongings. I never could have imagined that it would happen. I thought we were set for life. Then, I invested in Bernie Madoff's ponzi scheme." Pause. Silence. Deep breaths from everyone in the group. "Then," he went on, "I discovered that only the journey to the God-self within is really life-giving. I'm sorry it had to happen that way, but I'm better off now than I was then. I just didn't know it."

In every case, it was what people found on the other side of darkness that was the light for which they were seeking.

The death of one thing, it seems, is often a necessary part of the process of discovering where life really is for us. After we think that getting what we want is what it's all about, we discover that real life for us was, all this time, waiting for us somewhere else.

·⤞⤞⤞⤝⤝⤝·

When life turns dark
for us, we forget that
day always follows
the blackest part of night. In fact,
sometimes it is only the darkness
that propels us toward new light.

We hear over and over again that every
time one door closes, another one
opens. The problem is that they don't
tell us that to find it, we can't sit down
and quit. We have to walk through
the first door to get to the other.

It's not so much the future that is
the problem; it is anxiety about the
future that blocks us from dealing
well with the present. It's important
to be able to recognize endings;
otherwise, we will die in a past that
was never meant to be our future.

Being willing to begin again is one of life's greatest talents. There is nothing to be gained by refusing to move in another direction when this road clearly ends—except pain, of course.

When we learn to think big, to plan big, to reach for life beyond the present, we are most fully alive. "Hitch your wagon to a star," Ralph Waldo Emerson said. It's a ride worth taking even if we never get where we thought we wanted to go.

So often, we begin to see newly only when we can't see at all. It is only then that we are finally forced to create the ideas within us that we might otherwise never have bothered to consider at all.

When we don't know what to do next, that is exactly when we are best equipped to do something exciting. Then, the walls in our minds come down and anything is possible. Or as Faith Sullivan put it: "It was the sort of night when you think you could lie in the snow until morning and never get cold."

Regret does not happen because we did what we did. Regret comes because we did not do what we could have. And that awareness comes always with a twitch. It is an invitation without a response.

There are two approaches to life: one is attempting to fulfill all our desires; the other is learning to be desireless. Only one of these is certain.

Life is not one choice. It is a series of many choices. It is not one stage or phase or decision. It is many of them. And it is out of all those things that we become the fullness of ourselves. When we cut off our choices, we cut off another whole part of ourselves. "Where people fail," Anaïs Nin writes, "is that they elect a state and remain in it. This is a kind of death."

Doubt is the counterpoint of discovery. It is doubt of the enduring value of the present that leads us to the brink of discovery.

When questions are forbidden, doubt begins to erode our faith. "Doubt," Benjamin Jowett wrote, "comes in at the window when inquiry is denied at the door." Anything that cannot bear the light of a new question is to be considered very, very carefully.

God is the mystery no answers dare to determine. God is the mystery that makes all of life and our place in it, all our blunderings and all our changes, life-giving. Merry Christmas.

Doubt is the guardian of tomorrow. "Just think of the tragedy of teaching children not to doubt," the great lawyer Clarence Darrow said.

Otherwise, we would still be a land of slaves, an oppressor of women, a country without a justice system, and a land without courts.

Does religion ever doubt? Of course, it does. That's what theology is for. Otherwise, limbo would still be in the catechism of the church. Or as the philosopher Bertrand Russell put it: "In all affairs it's a healthy thing now and then to hang a question mark on the things you have long taken for granted."

·◦❯ 8 ❮◦·

*The universe is not required to be in
perfect harmony with human ambition.*
CARL SAGAN

A Place
Called "Home"

In each of us there is a place where we go in
the middle of chaos to escape from the fray.
It is that "home" place, that hiding place, that
soft place, where no memories of it come with
ragged edges and no thought of it is tinged
with fear. It's an empty beach, perhaps. Or a
hidden place on the bluff above town where

we remember being able to see everything while no one could see us.

For some it is the thought of the first blooming of a first garden. For others it is a secret spot under the back porch that smelled of clean earth. For many it's a hiding place in the basement or the shed or in a copse of trees along the road. It's that place to which we return in our minds to change life in the middle of too much life for us to take just then.

It is the place of our dreams and the hope of our hopes.

It's that natural place within us where the roar of the water or the silence of the mountains or the warmth of the desert or the moss of the swamp soothes our souls and makes us feel human again, at one with the universe again, in control again. Whatever it is, wherever it is, it calms us and makes us new. It was the place where we and nature became one.

For me, ironically, that special place was

right in the center of the city. In the very shadows of the city buildings lay a world beyond the world. It was the public dock on the bay of one of the Great Lakes, where tourists came to fish and sail and ride on a water taxi from the mainland over to the peninsula. Nothing more than a hotdog was ever sold there. There were no bands, no arcade games, no skateboard parks. It was commercially non-commercial. And yet it was my own small planet. There in that place everyone walked more slowly than usual, talked in more measured tones, dared to sit alone on the breakwall in total silence. There you could simply be yourself, no airs, no deadlines, no pressure, nothing false to serve or adore. Nothing that required us to bow down before it. There we just all melted into nature.

In our own day, when technology has trumped nature, we would do well to realize that those "home" places we all need and seek out in a time of the mechanical, the digital, the virtual, and the plastic are calling us to the center of our real selves. We must remember that it is the self for which we are seeking when we leave our worlds of glitz and glamour and sink into the real world. It is environment that shapes us and it is the natural to which we must cling when everyone else abandons it; if not, we lose the very soul of our lives.

To be out of touch with nature is to be out of touch with the self. The poet Homer talks about "his native home deep imag'd in his soul" as a way of reminding us that that which forms us never leaves us. It is we, however, who must continue the connections that formed us or else deny ourselves the fullness of the wisdom within us.

Environment is a subtle shaper of the self. It teaches us how to live. It is what we return to when the present does not provide what we need.

The real danger of the modern world is that it divorces the human being from nature, the very ground of what it is to be human. And so we run from thing to thing wondering why none of them rest us, refresh us, uplift us, bring us wonder anymore.

We are a people who "improve" on nature: We dig new lakes and fill with debris the ones that were there before us. We drill for oil under water and kill fish. We use chemicals to energize our land and pollute our skies. What's wrong with this picture?

We have taken charge of nature. The question is, have we improved on it? "The world is not to be put in order," Henry Miller wrote. "The world is order incarnate. It is for us to put ourselves in unison with this order."

Cities as a human environment, they say, are still an experiment. The question is whether or not the experiment is teaching us anything about how to live well; and, if so, in a world filled with starving children, is it working or not?

The Romantic poets of earlier ages wrote a great deal about "nature." We, on the other hand, hardly think of it. As a result, teachers tell us, schoolchildren in our cities no longer know where potatoes come from.

The relationship between nature and spirituality is a clear one: there is nothing like a good walk in the rain to produce both courage and humility in us.

The farther away we get from nature, the easier it has become for us to produce weapons that are capable of destroying it—and us with it, and all other living things. This we call "defense."

The more we lose a love, an intimacy, with nature, the less we value any life but human life. The problem is that a yearly trip to the zoo, the beach, or the backyard does not make a person a naturalist. We have to work at it.

Nature has no natural boundaries. It binds us from one side of the planet to the other, to the preservation of the globe and a universal respect for life. "Nature," Kathleen Raine writes, "is the common, universal language understood by all." Or at least it used to be.

There is a great spiritual struggle going on in the world today. It lies in the wrestling match between human holiness and the human arrogance that whispers to us that we can do anything we want to the earth and get away with it.

Here's a thought: Spend one day a month outdoors—go sit in the woods; take a book and have a picnic near a stream; plant a flower in a flower pot and tend it every day. Buy a puppy, a kitten, or a tiny parrot. Then watch what happens to you spiritually.

Think of it this way, Stanley Garn, anthropologist, says, "If the aborigine drafted an IQ test, all of Western civilization would presumably flunk it." Ouch.

I t isn't that our scientific, prefabricated, computerized world isn't affecting us. The problem is that it is. Our environment shapes us, fills us, makes us more or less real human beings.

A place that touches our heart forms us. Knowing what place has formed us, we can then decide what was missing from that place and needs to be provided, as well as what stayed with us from that place and needs to be maintained.

We are a people in transition. Always in transition. Always moving from place to place. We know that places mark us. But what if there is no place we can really call "home" because there have been so many of them?

There is no substitute for nature. It helps us to remember who and what we are not. Nature also enables us to understand who we are and what we must do to save it because of that.

·⁙ 9 ⁙·

Knowing others is wisdom.
Knowing the self is Enlightenment.
LAO TZU

Moments of Enlightenment

There are moments in life—both spiritual and intellectual—that are like no other. They change us. They redirect us. They complete us. Between these moments of Enlightenment—all of which are relatively rare—we simply go from one life event, one change point, to another. But after such times of acute insight, life takes on a different hue.

Enlightenment is a matter of coming to see life—to see ourselves—differently. It transforms us from average, everyday kinds of people to people with a purpose in life.

Sometimes it is the moment in life when we simply know, absolutely know, that the person we have just met is the person we are going to marry. Or sometimes it is the awareness that what we studied so hard to become is not what we are going to be. Or it might be the awareness that where I am is not where I belong. For me, it had to do with coming to understand that I would spend my entire life simply following the presence of God that consumed me more than anything else I could imagine in life. I dedicated my life to trying to unravel what that entailed in the present world and passing on those thoughts to others.

Where these moments of Enlightenment

come from can seldom be identified with any kind of certainty. They just are. They are within us, unspoken and often unseen, but never unknown. They strike us like lightning and burn within us all our lives. We recognize them when they happen to us, but we would never have planned them.

A moment of Enlightenment comes from outside ourselves and transforms us. It is not a plan; it's a happening. It fills us with new light. It astounds those around us to see us change our lives so suddenly, so totally. And in the end, it changes the focus, the direction, the very center of our lives.

·-3-3-3-6-6-6-·

E nlightenment requires complete abandonment of past certainties so that new possibilities can become possible.

When we open our hearts to life as it is rather than insist on life as we want it, we open our hearts to life yet to be lived.

There is a light within us that struggles for recognition. It is the dull and nagging awareness that we are not doing what we are meant to do.

Enlightenment, a change in spiritual perspective, comes suddenly but unfolds a bit at a time. We become accustomed to it in small portions.

When Enlightenment comes, a new certainty comes. When this new certainty comes, peace comes.

The Enlightened know the difference between what is important in life and what is merely good about it.

To be Enlightened is to care more about cultivating depth in life than simply expanding the breadth of it. It is easy to collect experiences; it is crucial to understand the meaning of them.

Appreciating what we have in a world more given to consumption than to joy is Enlightenment.

To be Enlightened does not mean that we never make mistakes. It means that we have the wisdom to realize that even mistakes have something to do with making us the best that we can be.

Enlightenment is what enables us to discriminate between what is fascinating and what is valuable. As Einstein says, "There are only two ways to live your life. One is as though nothing is a miracle. The other is as if everything is."

Don't be afraid to think differently than others do. Fear only that you will be closed to what the light in everyone else has to do with the quality of your own.

To be perfectly satisfied with who we are within is to be dark of soul. As Ralph Waldo Emerson puts it: "Though you may travel the world to find the beautiful, you must have it within you or you will find it not."

There is never the need to fear the darkness of evil when your own heart is full of the light of life.

When you can see possibility where others see nothing at all, that is Enlightenment.

Nothing created has been created without value. The Enlightened are those who are able to see what it is.

Enlightenment is coming to recognize the difference between what is worth the spending of a life and what is not. "There are many paths to enlightenment," Lao Tzu says. "Be sure to take one with a heart."

Life is full of miracles disguised as the ordinary. Enlightenment is the ability to see them in the commonplace.

Knowledge is not Enlightenment. Accruing information is a skill of the mind; Enlightenment, on the other hand, is a virtue of the soul.

It is possible to live forever in self-imposed darkness. Just by refusing to venture into the unknown idea, for instance, we can lock ourselves out of the fullness of life.

There is a different light in us all. We're born with it. When we release it within us, all the lights in the world around us shine even brighter themselves.

To be filled with the fire of life is to be grounded in goodness and freed by the spirit to do more than life would normally expect of us.

The Enlightened live life as if there was nothing more than what they can see and nothing greater than what they can't see.

The Enlightened are those who see through the darkness of the present moment to the values beyond it.

Enlightenment does not come for our own sake only. It comes so that we ourselves might be a light to others.

The Enlightened never worry about what happens. They know that what does happen in life will bring at least the same joy as what was hoped for—and probably more.